STUPID JOKES FOR CLEVER PEOPLE
&
CLEVER JOKES FOR STUPID PEOPLE

By
Tony Sandy

DragonEye Publishing

STUPID JOKES FOR CLEVER PEOPLE
&
CLEVER JOKES FOR STUPID PEOPLE
Copyrighted © 2017 by Tony Sandy

No part of this book may be reproduced in any form or by any electronic or mechanical means including information storage and retrieval systems, without permission in writing from the author with the only exception being a reviewer who may quote short excerpts in a review.

First Edition
First printing April 1, 2017
ISBN 13: 978-1-61500-144-6 (Paperback)
ISBN 13: 978-1-61500-100-2 (EPub ebook)
ISBN 13: 978-1-61500-180-4 (PDF)

Library of Congress Control Number: 2017937240

Published by Jokorama, an Imprint of DragonEye Publishing

DragonEye Publishing
753 Linden Place, Unit A
Elmira, NY 14901

www.DragonEyePublishers.com
Contact: Orders@DragonEyePublishers.com

STUPID JOKES FOR CLEVER PEOPLE
&
CLEVER JOKES FOR STUPID PEOPLE

What the critics have said

'This book should be a roaring success – especially if you throw it at the back of an open fire!'

'Once I picked up this book, I found it hard to put down - it had superglue on the back cover'

'This man has one of the finest comic brains in the business – he keeps it in a jar under his bed'

'This book will walk off the shelves – it'll have to as no-one will pick it up'

'This book will change your life forever but not in a pleasant way'

'This writer should go far – preferably Siberia'

'The perfect gift to give, to people you hate'

'This book has gone viral – hence the slightly tacky feel of the cover, sprayed with germ killer'

'This man should not have been allowed back into the community' (my psychiatrist)

STUPID JOKES FOR CLEVER PEOPLE
&
CLEVER JOKES FOR STUPID PEOPLE

INTRODUCTION

(There is no introduction)

- I lied

STUPID JOKES FOR CLEVER PEOPLE
&
CLEVER JOKES FOR STUPID PEOPLE

INTRODUCTION

If you don't understand a joke, it's not funny. Alternatively, if you do and don't want to, it's also not funny but for a different reason. If we see something as offensive or insulting, it's because we don't want to be associated with it: For us, it has a personal meaning, which we'd rather not be reminded of thank you very much and so go into an automatic, paranoid defence reaction, in order to block it out of our conscious awareness. If we see it as a joke, it's because we interpret it as meaningless, harmless, non-embarrassing – that is we don't fear it as disclosure of our personal life or history.

You have to speak a language and understand it's cultural heritage, to laugh at a joke. Only slapstick is universal humour because it is visual (composed of body language) and emotional (tone of voice indicators).

A good joke hides the punchline, so that you are surprised by its revelation – much as you would be if you accidentally stumbled over a cliff edge but with less permanent damage.

STUPID JOKES FOR CLEVER PEOPLE
&
CLEVER JOKES FOR STUPID PEOPLE

PREFACE

If you like a mixture of the crudity of Two and a Half Men, Steve Wright's surreal logic, The Goons insanity, plus the odd bit of black humour and terrible, terrible puns then this is the book for you!

STUPID JOKES FOR CLEVER PEOPLE
&
CLEVER JOKES FOR STUPID PEOPLE

CONTENTS PAGE

I'm not content and haven't been in years, so why would you expect there to be a 'contents' page?

AN IRISH LETTER

Dear Wills

I'm not sure if I'm going to write this letter or not, so if you don't get it, that's why (Write and let me know in either case).

I don't know what the weather is like there but it is the same here. By the way we might come up there on holiday. If I don't see you when I arrive, it's because I've decided not to come. We were going to visit last year too but as you hadn't moved to where you are now because you were somewhere else, there didn't seem much point. How's the wife? No, not yours, mine (If you can see her from there, you've got bloody good eyes!). We were abroad last year - The Paris Hilton! We even talked to her but she didn't recognise me, even though we'd never met.

As I lay here writing this letter, I see Mary is in bed beside me, which is strange as my wife is called Alice. Oh yes, now I remember - it's my cousin Mick's wife, who's come to visit and I'm in the wrong bedroom again. My eyes are not what they used to be - I think they used to be my armpits, which could explain why my sight stinks. Children grow up so quick nowadays. Last week, Donald my eldest, was fifteen and this week he's sixteen (Birthdays - who'd have them, except people who are older).

STUPID JOKES FOR CLEVER PEOPLE & CLEVER JOKES FOR STUPID PEOPLE

My mother would like to say something but as she's tied and gagged in the garage, that would be difficult. We tried to give her a respray, so we could get her deported as one of those illegal immigrants (She always wanted to see the Taj Mahal, so we thought it would be a nice Christmas Present for her but she wouldn't hear of it. 'You're too generous son,' was all she said as I dragged her screaming and kicking outside. 'No Turkey for you this year!' I said (or India for that matter)). 'Now where's that spade?' (She always wanted to be buried beside my father but I think she was expecting to be dead first. Still nowadays, you can't always get what you want). Must go now. Someone is knocking at the door and I think it is the police collecting for Charity and as she isn't here, I'll have to answer the door myself.

Your friend

Pope Pius, The Tenth (only kidding - Pope Pius, The Eleventh!). No I'm fibbing again, it's just me as you'll recognise from the photo I didn't send.

STUPID JOKES FOR CLEVER PEOPLE
&
CLEVER JOKES FOR STUPID PEOPLE

COMPARISONS

A hand is better than a woman
because it never gets a headache
never threatens to go back to its mother
never gets a period
never gets pregnant
never gives you the clap
never sues you for alimony
never berates your performance
never expects flowers or chocolates
never cares that you go out drinking with your mates
never locks you out after an argument
never wants to move to Sacramento
etc

A hand is better than a man
because it doesn't go to sleep afterwards
and will make you a cup of tea
doesn't slobber all over you when drunk
doesn't sleep with another woman then lie about it
doesn't give you the clap
doesn't go in the other room when you start crying about the death of Bambi
doesn't ignore all your friends, except the ones he wants to sleep with
doesn't wake you in the middle of the night for it, when you've got to go to work in the morning
doesn't smell like an open sewer etc.

STUPID JOKES FOR CLEVER PEOPLE
&
CLEVER JOKES FOR STUPID PEOPLE

DITTIES

Men stink, drink and think
Women scheme, scream and dream

'Okay men, fire at Will!'
'Why me, I've done you no ill!'

The cannons roar
The bullets fly
- careful with that stick
You nearly poked me in the eye!

'Cap'n Ahab, we've spotted
the great white nose!'
'Okay lads, fire the harpoon
- thar she blows!'

Oh look, there's Aphrodite
and she's not wearing a nightie!

Robin Hood, Robin Hood
Riding through the glen
Robin Hood, Robin Hood
pursued by his men
- he stole all their money
and they didn't find it funny!
Robbing Hood, Robbing Hood
Robbing Hood...

STUPID JOKES FOR CLEVER PEOPLE
&
CLEVER JOKES FOR STUPID PEOPLE

Robin Hood, Robin Hood
Riding through the glen
Robin Hood, Robin Hood
With his band of men
Feared by the good
Loved by the bad!
Robin's Mad, Robin's mad
Robin's mad......

Roses are red
Violets are blue
Mine are Green
'coz they fell in the stew

Roses are red
Violets are blue
Mine are pink
Are yours too?

Roses are red
Violence is blue
If you don't shut up
I'm going to strangle you!

STUPID JOKES FOR CLEVER PEOPLE
&
CLEVER JOKES FOR STUPID PEOPLE

JOKES

2 Glaswegians were taking the ashes of a friend home, when one of them dropped it and burst into tears.
'Take it easy Jimmy, there's no point crying over spilled Malc.'

Say Paddy why are you looking up into that oak and why were you earlier staring intently at that sycamore and that there elm?'
'Ah well, me mother told me when I was a boy that good things come in trees and I'm just checking.'

"Where are you going on holiday Dave?"
"Narnia, what do you mean Narnia?"
"Narnia your bloody business is it?"

Rolf Harris was asked what he thought was the best thing about his portrait of the queen?
He said "I don't know really?" then he hummed and he hahed, and he hummed and he hahed.

Just before he died, Peter Sellers was bitten on the neck by a vampire. Professor Van Helsing, hearing of this, immediately rushed to his graveside,
Digging open the casket, he opened up the lid, when a voice piped up inside
"Is that you Spike?"
"Well, sort of"
Thud!

STUPID JOKES FOR CLEVER PEOPLE
&
CLEVER JOKES FOR STUPID PEOPLE

A girl had her pet amphibian eaten by a passing wild dog in the Australian outback, when she spotted the same animal captured and on display in a pet shop. She went up to the assistant and asked for her pet back, saying she only wanted what the dog had eaten or to put it another way-
'How much is that froggy in the dingo, the one with the waggily tail?'

It was exam time and Richard, the freckle faced fifties throw back, was up against his fellow geeks, whose parents were equally as old fashioned as he was and who lived on either side of his house - Matthews and Harris. After the results came through, it was discovered that he'd done extremely well but the other two had only done half as well as expected: In fact you could say that the square with the spotty nose, was equal to the sons of the squares on the other two sides.

'Hey little girl, do you want to see my Willy?'
'Oh yes please!'
'Willy!"
'Yes Dad?'
'There's a little girl to see you!"

A famous but arrogant composer of operas was sitting in his favourite armchair, reading the paper, when in came his wife.
'You lazy bastard, I don't know why I ever married you! You do absolutely nothing around the house!'
'Be quiet woman, can't you see I am Bizet!'

STUPID JOKES FOR CLEVER PEOPLE
&
CLEVER JOKES FOR STUPID PEOPLE

Do you think I'm homosexual?'
'What makes you ask?'
'I love Jack Daniels and I'm very fond of Johnny Walker'

A Dalek got a job in a health spa and was asked on its first day what it knew about skin?
"I- can- fry- it- to- a- crisp!"
"Excellent - here's your first customer!"
"Exfoliate, exfoliate!"

A plane crashed and the two survivors scrambled out. One was totally okay but the other had a big gash in his arm.
'Would you like me to sew up that wound for you?'
'No, I did a course on DIY surgery'
'Okay - suture yourself!'

Jesus was passing a furniture warehouse, when he saw two men arguing about who had the right to put their chair in as there was only space for one.
"Rabbi, which of us deserves to have our way?"
Looking at the situation for a while, Jesus thought then said
"Ah I know! Let he who is without sin, stow the first throne!"

Groucho Marx visited a VD clinic for his results
'I'm sorry Mr Marx but you've definitely caught something'
'What should I do?'

'Well first, we need to trace whoever might have given it to you, to warn them they may have got it too'
'Yes of course doctor!'
At this he races outside and starts singing up and down the streets -
'Lydia oh Lydia, have you seen Lydia? The lady who gave me Chlamydia - the VD infested lady?'

St Michael was sending recruits down to Earth to get reincarnated as human beings
"Who are you?"
"I am to be a woman"
"Blessed are you my sister - go forth and multiply!"
"And who are you?"
"I'm a politician"
"Say shouldn't you be coming up from the other place, rather than dropping down from here? No? Oh well, your mission is to go to Earth and sow the seeds of discontent - go forth and divide the populace amongst itself and subtract its numbers. You are there to keep its numbers down"
"Who are you?"
"I'm to be an accountant"
"Your mission is to go to Earth thinking logic and reasoning will sort out its problems but sadly you'll soon find out that nothing adds up down there"

The dead grandmother of a Vietnamese boat person, was shipped over to the US but not before

her body was preserved through mummification, which included the removal of her internal organs to slow down the process of decay. Her grandson, who worked in a lazer lab, decided to take 3-D images of the corpse to show other relatives, who also lived in the States. Unfortunately on his way home, he was pulled over by a female member of the Highway Patrol, who asked him why he was crying and what he was holding in his hand?
"It's a hologram of my hollow nan from Vietnam but it's a sham as she's come out looking like boiled ham, mam"

One sunny day in early 2009, an old man approached the White House from across Pennsylvania Avenue, where he had been sitting on a park bench. He said to the Marine guard at the gate 'I would like to go in and meet President Bush please.' The Marine looked at the old timer and said, 'Sir, Mr Bush is no longer President, so he no longer resides here.' The old man said 'okay' and walked away.

The following day, the same man approached the White House and asked the same Marine: 'Could I go in and see President Bush?' The Marine replied: 'Sir, as I told you yesterday, Mr Bush is no longer President, so he isn't here any more.' The man thanked him again and walked away.
On the third day, the elderly man repeated the performance and the same Marine looked somewhat agitated as he explained to him, loudly

and clearly: 'Look, Sir, this is the third day in a row that you have come here asking to speak to Mr Bush, and this is the third day in a row that I have had to tell you that Mr Bush is no longer President and no longer lives here. Can't you understand that?' 'Oh, I understand all right,' the man said. 'I just love hearing it.' The Marine snapped to attention, saluted and said: 'See you tomorrow, Sir.'

'Do you know that in the Far East they've got kidnapping down to a fine art'
'Really?'
'Yeh, everybody has their specific task'
'What are those guys over there doing?'
'They're writing the ransom notes'
'And those guys over there?'
'They drive the getaway cars'
'And those ones over there with the string?'
'Oh, they're the Thais that bind'

'Doctor, doctor! Mr Wilson has escaped and taken a plane to a foreign country, with the intention of throwing himself in the nearest river!'
'Is he insane?'
'No but he might be in denial.'

Karen Carpenter was in the garden when first one, then two, three, four birds etc. of a particular species started cropping up. Then she noticed her brother out of the corner of her eye and put two and two together. Turning to him she exclaimed:-

STUPID JOKES FOR CLEVER PEOPLE
&
CLEVER JOKES FOR STUPID PEOPLE

'Wydoo birds suddenly appear, when you're near
Just like me, they long to be, close to you'

A man was walking his dog when another man
passed him as he was picking up the dogs business
in a plastic bag.
 "Gee that's pleasant!"
 "It's not so bad but my memory is going"
 "Why is that a problem"
 "I sometimes forget what bag my sandwiches are
in"

 An oriental gentleman is doing a crossword, when
he got stuck on a clue
 "What's another word for variations?"
 "Fluctuations"
 "Fluck you too - I was only asking!"

Tony Christie of the group Dawn, decided to go on
a metal work course. He decided to specialise in
making monkeys. Working on his biggest project
so far, he turned to his tutor and said "I'm having
real difficulty with this ape and I'm not sure of my
technique - is this the way to hammer gorilla's?"

'Before we shoot you as a spy, you Germanic
bastard, do you mind if we splash you with eau-de-
cologne?'
'Yes, you English Pig-dog! You can take Horst to
slaughter but you cannot make him stink!'

STUPID JOKES FOR CLEVER PEOPLE
&
CLEVER JOKES FOR STUPID PEOPLE

A man tried to contact an old friend, who'd moved back to China. After 6 goes he slammed down the phone.
'What's wrong?' his wife asked
'Every time I try to get Frank Choi, all I get is a Wong number!'

"Remind me not to go to the miners drop in centre ever again!"
"Why?"
"I fell down the shaft and broke both my legs"

A man walked into his hotel room and immediately threw Mick Jagger off the balcony.
"What the hell did you do that for!"
" See I told, there's no way this place is a stones throw from the beach!"

A streaker runs onto the football pitch, before finally being brought down by the goalkeeper's from both sides. The headline in the following days paper read 'Streaker grabbed by the goalies'

The kings son was upset at the thought of the previous kingdom's before theirs, destruction.
'Sadly son' said his father 'into each life some reigns must fall'

The speaker of The House of Commons was asked to get meals in for MPs, with regards to a paper being debated overnight. He walked into The Chamber with the first course, at a point where a

STUPID JOKES FOR CLEVER PEOPLE
&
CLEVER JOKES FOR STUPID PEOPLE

heated argument had broken out.
He shouted at them -
'Hors d'eouvres, hors d'eouvres!'

Schrodinger was arguing with another physicist about his famous cat, when his fellow scientist asked, if it was something else, would the experiment still work?
'Now you're splitting hares and wanting me to pull a rabbit out of the box!'

'What's that in your pocket?'
'Mud'
'Mud?'
'Not just mud – it's soil from my favourite Spanish football club's grounds'
'How do you know it isn't fake?'
'Oh it's real Madrid for sure'

Once upon a time both men and women were equally attractive, until one day the males of the species started blowing their tops because they were losing their beauty sleep and they've been turning ugly ever since.

A man went for a dump in the woods. When he came out again, he was followed by a grizzly.
Some guy shouted
'Look out – bear behind!'
'Don't be silly! I made sure I pulled my trousers up!'

STUPID JOKES FOR CLEVER PEOPLE
&
CLEVER JOKES FOR STUPID PEOPLE

What's the dilemma faced by every woman, when faced with the choice of sticking to their diet or eating a cream cake?
'Tubby or not tubby, that is the question!'

A friend was trying to contact Jonah on his mobile, when he got a recorded message
'Hi, I'm not able to take your call right now as I'm in whales but I'll get back to you as soon as possible.'

Two undertakers were moving remains from a crematorium, when they crashed into each other. Hugh Grant's ashes and those of a famous inventor being reinterred, got mixed up, so that you couldn't tell who's Hugh and what's Watt

A bunny-boiler stalked a man she was obsessed with.
'I love you – why don't you marry me?'
'I don't even know you – go away!'
'Well if you change your mind, just give me a ring!'

A slippery customer with an even slipperier solicitor, was arrested by the police the other day. They were so afraid of losing him that they rushed the case through the legal system. It was caught to court in fifty seconds flat!

'I found a dead rat in the toilet. It had been there for weeks. You don't mind me telling you all the

gory details, do you?'
'No, I bet you're just glad to get it out of your cistern'

'Inspector, somebody just broke into Notre Dame cathedral!'
'Do you have any suspects?'
'Have you heard of somebody called Quasimodo?'
'No, the name doesn't ring a bell?'

'I've got insomnia. The doctor thinks I should take some pills but my wife thinks I should try a herbal remedy. What should I do?'
'Sleep on it'

'What do you want to be when you grow up son?'
'I've half a mind to become a brain surgeon'
Well you'll need a whole one to get that job'

A man entered a psychiatric unit looking for the head honcho. He walked up to a man wearing a white coat.
'Are you in charge round here?'
'No, I'm a frayed knot'

Two Celts were out hunting one night, when one spotted an enemy coming towards them, out of the distance. He ran back to his compatriot, shouting 'Quick, run for it! There's a Roman in the gloomin!'

STUPID JOKES FOR CLEVER PEOPLE
&
CLEVER JOKES FOR STUPID PEOPLE

Two birdwatchers were out twitching
'Is that a mallard over there?'
'Eider-'
'That's not an Eider!'
'-I'der a duck once'

A gangster wanted to get rid of his East European rival, so he put a contract out on him. The killer dumped the body in wet cement, on a motorway flyover. He emailed the gangster to let him know the hit had been successful. All he wrote was 'The Czech is in the post'

Freddie Mercury started being a nuisance to his mum, when he threw down and smashed a plate, saying he was bored. When she ignored him, he threw down another.
'Enough Freddie or God will punish you!'
'No he won't – God knows I want to break free!'

A Vietnamese monk was discussing the nature of reality with his farmer friend, when he decided enough was enough and stormed off into a field. Suddenly the farmer shouted after him and he thought he'd won the argument, until he stood on an explosive and was blown to bits.
'It's all mined!' was what he'd shouted
'What makes you stand here in the rain and snow for hours? I've stood and watched you from my window for ages.
'Fortitude'
'Fortitude?'

STUPID JOKES FOR CLEVER PEOPLE
&
CLEVER JOKES FOR STUPID PEOPLE

'Yes, fortitude' and with that he pulled out a club and hit the man on the head.
'Forty-freed,' he said to himself.

Princess Leia walked into a bar
'Yoda!'
'You drunked idiot! Do I look like that shrunked misfit?'
'Yoda!'
'If Luke Skywalker was here you wouldn't speak to me like that!'
'Don't you recognize me? It's your old boyfriend, Han Solo! Yoda lady, Yoda lady that rocks me!'

Why do men want to throw, kick or catch spherical objects? I personally can't stand ball games! On second thoughts, scratch that.

I went up to the spirits counter of my local supermarket but it looked deserted
'Is there anybody there?' I asked
'Knock once for yes, twice for no.'

When the work party returned to the prison camp, led by the lazy guard, nobody was surprised that prisoners were missing – in fact it was a four-gone conclusion.

I'm not very good at business. Firstly my fruit market stall went pear shaped, then my plumbing company went down the pan. On top of this my boat building firm sunk withoput trace, quickly followed by my canoe shop disappearing without a paddle. I finally thought I'd made it out of the decline, when I joined the diet industry but even that bottomed out

A man was walking his dog, when it stopped and did its business on the grass. A man suddenly appeared and asked 'Are you going to pick that up?'
'It's diarrhoea – do you think I'm going to suck it up with a straw?'

'Chief Sitting Bull, do you think it's fair that the Indian Nations are being paid welfare by The United States government?'
'Yes but I do have reservations'

Norman Wisdom died and went to heaven, getting a job in The Angel of Death's shop. Every January, he could be seen walking the streets, carrying a sandwich board and chanting
'Mr Grim's sale! Mr Grim's sale!'

Prince Philip was being shown round a fish farm, when he slipped and fell into a salmon pen. He was dragged out soaking wet. The manager of the place fussed and flustered around him.
One of the worker's said 'I don't know what he's so worried about it – it's just water off a duke's back.'

Police became concerned that Paul Simon was still living in his parents house, despite being old and wealthy. The judge had a court injunction put on him – fifty days to leave your mother!

A man is being shown round a pharmaceuticals company, when he suddenly notices a cog pick up a test tube, pour some of the contents into a flask and look at the results. He turned to his companion and said "Isn't that remarkable?'
'Oh that? It's just a lab technician.'

'What's this about you living on the streets John?'
'It's true. We got rid of our old phone and got one of those new fangled smart phones. We had a fire at the house and by the time I'd worked out how to dial 999, the place had burnt down.'

A man went to Hong Kong looking for a Chinese friend, who hadn't been able to speak since birth. Visiting his last known address, he asked various people if they knew him. Every time he put down his battered suitcase, he received the same reply 'No dumb Ping here, mister!'

'Jack, Jack!'
'What is it Tom?'
'They're doing terrible things down at the sweet factory!'
'What do you mean?'
'They're using those mosquitoes in their confectionary – the ones that hang about the nut trees.'
'Nuts?'
'No, you idiot! Gnats, gnats; whole hazel gnats!

Cadbury's bake them, then cover them in chocolate!'

I saw a man talking to himself on the street the other day.
I said 'Only crazy people talk to themselves.'
'What did you say?'
'I wasn't talking to you.'

The head of MI5 thought that The Gruffalo would make a good saboteur, so cloned and genetically modified it. Versions one to six, types A to E, were failures but it was decided to have one last go at improving its intelligence. Alas 7D was also a failure. Calling in his team of boffins, he angrily banged on the desk
'Gruffalo seven is dumb-D dumb, dumb-dumb; dumb-D, dumb dumb; D-D, D-D-D!'

I can't stand all this conspiracy nonsense about Lady Diana Spencer. The royal family welcomed her with open arms. I often heard them chanting her name in
unison, every time she appeared
"Lady, die! Lady, die!! Lady, die!!!"

I invited some friends round the other night for a meal. I was working on the first course, imbibing some wine as I was going along, when one of them came up to me and enquired
'Pistou?'
'No but I'm getting there'

THE SHERLOCK SERIES

'What do you make of this gigantic footprint Watson?'
'Search me Holmes!'
'I'll give you a clue. Notice the tartan pattern on the sole'
' - you don't mean"
'Yes Watson, old chum - this was made by a member of the ancient Caledonian race!'
'Great Scot, a great Scot!'

'Watson, what do you get if you cross the middle three letters of the alphabet with a many branched, botanical wonder?'
'I don't know Holmes'
'It's L-M-N tree my dear fellow!'

Sherlock Holmes was investigating a case where the victim had, had his head smashed in by a rock.
'Watson, looking at the wound, what can you tell me about the weapon used to dispatch the victim?'
'Well it was blunt and could have been made of anything as far as I can see'
'Then you didn't note the sand on his forehead, where the blow had been struck?'
'No, I don't see the significance - it could be a stone I suppose!'
'It's not just stone - it's sedimentary my dear Watson!'

Holmes was invited to a family reunion and took Watson along with him.
'You know my brother Mycroft of course and his work for the Home Office. Over there is my cousin, who is something in the city'
'Oh?'
'Yes, he has a reputation for dealing in financial matters, which shows as keen a mind as mine and my brother's'
'Do I know him?'
'How can you not have heard of Shylock Holmes?'

'Watson, do you see that man over there, who seems to be glowing?'
'Yes old bean'
'He works in the uranium mining industry and is Scottish'
'How do you know that old fellow?'
'Because every Macleod has a silver lining'

THE DAVE SERIES

'When I said give Jimmy Johnson both barrels Dave, I meant of the beer he'd ordered'

'When I said deck the halls Dave, I meant decorate the place, not beat the shit out of Phil and Jane'

'What have I told you about smoking fish Dave? Not while at work, now stub it out and do what I pay you for.'

THE BAR TENDER SERIES

A man walks into a bar and notice a bottle of whisky, rattling around on the shelf. So he asks the bartender "What's that?"
 "Oh, that's just a restless spirit"
 "And what about that bottle floating in mid air?"
 "It's just a little high spirited"

 Another man walks into the same bar.
 "Give me a shot of red eye!"
 Bang! The bartender knocks him flying.
 "Say what did you give me a black eye for?"
 "We ain't got no red eye

Guy walks into a bar looking for a local hoodlum called Johnny Mashtik
 "You seen Mashtik tonight?", he asked the bar keeper
 "He was here a minute ago - no, wait he must have gone out when my back was turned"

ONE LINERS / SHORT JOKES

If the world is constantly changing, the question naturally arises - what the flux going on?

Why is that when reality breaks down, you can never find a quantum mechanic?

Heisenberg's uncertainty principle rules...maybe

Do retired Gynaecologists like to keep their hand in?

As every five year old child will tell you – squashed rabbit, it's just not bunny anymore

I live in a house with three other manic-depressives. It's just a typical two up, two down kind of place

Half a dozen pigeons landed on my head the other day.
I thought 'Silly Flockers!'

I went into a shop the other day. The girl behind the counter asked if I wanted a little bag. I said no thank you, I'm already married.

My wife and I employ East European attitudes towards cleaning. Mine is check and slow vacuuming, while she's always Russian through house work.

STUPID JOKES FOR CLEVER PEOPLE
&
CLEVER JOKES FOR STUPID PEOPLE

Police like jumpers - they're always pointing and shouting at drivers 'Pullover!'

I'm worried about my wife. She keeps asking for TLC – Troubling Lesbian Contact.

Supermarkets in France - Je queues!

A crime writer inherited some land from a dead relative. He of course sold it off in plots.

King Charles had dandruff - I bet he's missing his head and shoulders now!

Old bikers never die - they just get recycled

Sir Ranulph Fiennes was trudging through the Antarctic, when his companion asked him what the temperature was. Looking down at his toes, he said
'Minus two'

My wife says I'm like one of those chewy sweets – a worthless original

Did you hear about the angry chef, who gave his wife an artichoke?

If you only complete part of a ski run, does that mean you were only half piste?

'Mum, what's a Didgeridoo?'

STUPID JOKES FOR CLEVER PEOPLE
&
CLEVER JOKES FOR STUPID PEOPLE

'Whatever it damn well pleases I suppose'

People from England don't believe me, when I tell them that the Sun comes out nearly everyday in Scotland but then so does the Express and the Mail

The East Enders murder had Morse dashing after Dot

What do you a call a woman that takes all your money and leaves you out to dry?
Peg

What do you get if you advertise for people with a particular surname, to turn up at your house on a particular date? I don't know but it sounds like a load of Pollacks.

In the British Army it's eyes right, salute the flag. In the American Army it's 'I's right, you's wrong dick head!'

I told my wife she looked like a model. She smiled. I meant a Model-T

'Mick, what are you doing with that Greek pastry stuck to your head?'
'Well Patrick, I always fancied getting one of them Baclava helmets myself.'

'My hat just blew off!'
'Did it say pardon?'

STUPID JOKES FOR CLEVER PEOPLE
&
CLEVER JOKES FOR STUPID PEOPLE

UFOs are made in Scotland from girders,
according to Irn Bru but only Smarties have the
answer!

I tried putting myself in my wife's shoes the other
day but they were too tight and she
told me to get out of her dress as well

'Why are you firing at the river Frank?'
'Someone told me it would be fun but I dunno
what's so good about shooting rapids?'

A master sergeant was laying on his bunk reading,
when a cat jumped up on his bedside table and
crapped on his personal possessions. He jumped
up and screamed.
'Not on my watch!'

A nervous young man went up to his dad and said
he wanted to be a stand up comedian
'You, a comic? Don't make me laugh!'

A hobbit went for a haircut.
'I want a short back and sides,
'I thought you'd already got that'

Dai came out of the pit, complaining about his
back. Going to the doctor, he asked what was
wrong.
'Oh nothing serious, it's just a miner problem'

STUPID JOKES FOR CLEVER PEOPLE
&
CLEVER JOKES FOR STUPID PEOPLE

'Mum, do I have to eat this lettuce?'
'Yes'
'Why?'
'Cos I say so'

If love makes the world go round, does hate make it go square?

I hate messy, femaile dogs. Everywhere they go, they litter

Aren't people generous? When I worked in a dry cleaners, people would give me the shirts off their back

I bought a turkey for Christmas – they don't make decent films nowadays

There are two types of people in the world – those who write dribble like this and those who read it

I saw a sign on a boat the other day. It said 'For Sale.'
You can't fool me – there aren't any sails on a motorboat!

I had a German girlfriend once. She was hard as nails. Her name was Gerda

As geneticists will tell you – you cannot make an egg without breaking omelettes

STUPID JOKES FOR CLEVER PEOPLE
&
CLEVER JOKES FOR STUPID PEOPLE

When I got married, my wife made a happy man very poor

Dragon's Den – life's a pitch, then your business dies

Erotic art? I've seen the writhing on the walls!

Sir Bob Geldorf was asked why hunting should be banned
 'The answer is obvious, for fox sake!'

Notice on office door : Assassination Bureau – we aim to please

I wanted to be a landscape gardener but I didn't see any fuschia in it

If you put weedkiller on a Welshman, why doesn't it matter?
Because he's boyo-degradable

Golfer in a bunker
'Fore! Damn, missed it again!
Five! Soddit!
Six...'

'Are you in there?'
'No'
'Then who answered?'
'Me, myself and I'
I went to a funeral home the other day. It was

STUPID JOKES FOR CLEVER PEOPLE
&
CLEVER JOKES FOR STUPID PEOPLE

closed because of a bereavement

I'm sixty but I feel the same as when I was a child – miserable, depressed and pissed off with life!

Did you hear about the pop fan, who had a lucky escape? She wasn't seriously injure,d even though she fell over a cliff

There are two types of people in the world – those that agree with me and those that are wrong

'I'm new to duelling'
'Never mind. Give it your best shot'

I couldn't decide if I wanted to be a heating engineer or not, I kept blowing hot and cold

When I told my friends that a clumsy idiot like me was going to become a pastry chef, they all laughed but the choux is on the other foot now!

John Steed needed a date for the night. Cathy Gale turned him down, so he phoned Tara King. She was busy. He then found himself in a quandry.
'Should I call Purdey or dial-Emma?'

I went to the shop for some evaporated milk but it had vanished off the shelf
What did Henry the eighth say to his second wife, when planning a trip?

STUPID JOKES FOR CLEVER PEOPLE
&
CLEVER JOKES FOR STUPID PEOPLE

'Right Anne, it's time to head off'

'Get your bloody dog away from my cap!'
'I don't like your attitude!'
'It isn't your hat-he-chewed but mine

I speak Flemish but I won't when my cold clears up

How many philosophers does it take to change a lightbulb?
None because there is no empirical proof that philosophy actually exists

Did you hear about the prostitute that specialized in clerical gents?
She could do a hundred revs a minute

If you're looking for an epileptic in a clothing store, where are you most likely to find him?
In the fitting room

What do you say to a mountain, with nice legs?
That's a lovely Pyrenees you've got

'I've got one of those small greyhound type dogs but it won't do what I say. Any ideas?'
'Whippet?'
'That's a bit harsh!'

My girlfriend owns a tazer – she's a real stunner!

STUPID JOKES FOR CLEVER PEOPLE
&
CLEVER JOKES FOR STUPID PEOPLE

'Who's that bloke under the steamroller Jack?'
'Oh him, he's just my flat mate'

A lot of women hope to marry a man who is filthy rich but most end up with one who is just filthy

The old anti-communist league have now started an anti-literacy campaign
Better dead than read.

A man broke into a pet shop and stole all the dog restraints.
Police are looking for leads

I really like you deep down - say about 6 foot.

To some people 'Hi Jean!' is just a greeting to a friend

Sausages - what's the wurst that can happen?

I will repay saith The Lord!(I just need a little more time, things haven't been easy lately).

The grandeur that was Rome - the glory that is greasy fish and chips!

Become a professional body piercer today - join the army and get some bayonet practice in

Why did the testicles not like being confined in underwear?

STUPID JOKES FOR CLEVER PEOPLE
&
CLEVER JOKES FOR STUPID PEOPLE

Because they preferred hanging out together

Girls don't make passes at snakes in grasses

Stealing is the sincerest form of flattery

What good are disabled toilets? I want one that works!

Our new car has a sign on it 'Safety belts must be worn'
Wouldn't it be better if they were new and in good repair?

We had a ninetieth birthday surprise party for my uncle Tom last week - the biggest surprise was he died the year before

People often tell me to chillaxe but they forget I'm a serial killer

I like cottage pie but I find the bricks hard to chew

As I said to the hangman 'Sometimes it's not good to be in the loop.'

I'm such a lazy bastard that when I entered the Try-athlon, I came last

Just remember that although hate sees all, louvres are blinds
If you're a slave the yokes on you!

STUPID JOKES FOR CLEVER PEOPLE
&
CLEVER JOKES FOR STUPID PEOPLE

First thing in the morning I'm only half human. Fortunately for my wife, it's not the bottom half

The first time I proposed to my wife, I went down on one knee – I wasn't expecting a right hook as an answer

I work in counter intelligence – I'm on the help desk at B&Q

I never realized that when I became a surgical assistant, I'd have my work cut out for me

My wife is like a depressed sea mammal – she wails and blubbers all day long

I'm not really into Arthurian legend but I do find Merlot the magician fascinating

It seems that you can marry a pig in Islam but not eat one

I hate bent coppers! You can't get them in the slot machines

A man attacked me the other day for chewing my biro. I put it down to pen top aggression

Thieves broke into Lidl at the weekend. Only one item was taken. Police believe it was stollen
My son has got green fingers. I told him to use a hankerchief but would he listen?

STUPID JOKES FOR CLEVER PEOPLE
&
CLEVER JOKES FOR STUPID PEOPLE

Did you know that men have an erection when asleep? That's so they can feel a dick head at night as well as during the day

A Virgin plane was on a runway, when Ryan Air landed on top of it. It's not a virgin now

I thought mutton was ba food, until I tried Smirnoff

My dog has got three ears. We call him Spot the difference

'I thought you said you'd watched your weight all your life?'
'I have. I've watched it grow, and grow, and grow...

I have the strength of six men! Unfortunately they're all fat, lazy bastards

A flying saucer landed in my herb garden. I knew it was an alien abduction case as there was missing thyme

I taught my wife to fly. I threw her out of the plane at twenty thousand feet

I crept up on a log the other day. It didn't hear me as it was fast asleep
Is gallows humour only for the highly strung?

STUPID JOKES FOR CLEVER PEOPLE
&
CLEVER JOKES FOR STUPID PEOPLE

I'm such a failure that if I threw myself off a cliff I'd miss

I drove my wife into the arms of another man. She wanted to take a taxi but I thought I owed her that much

Why do I always get the blame for everything, even though I'm clearly guilty?

A vampire wanted to go out with a zombie girl but her father objected
'Over my dead body!'

'I hate these people who go around showing off their fancy camera equiment'
'You're not into flash photography then?'

I went into a sweet shop. The girl behind the counter was up a ladder. I wanted to ask her if she had a particular bar but from where I was, I could see she didn't have any Snickers

'What do you do at Selfridges?'
'Sell fridges'
'Yes, that was what I was asking – what do you do at Selfridges?'

A man walked up and patted a woman's dog, then started scratching himself
'Has your dog got fleas?'
'No'

STUPID JOKES FOR CLEVER PEOPLE
&
CLEVER JOKES FOR STUPID PEOPLE

'Well it has now'

'I thought you said, you wanted to see your uncle Jack but you never said a blind word, the entire time we were there'
'See him, yes but speak to him, no'

I wonder if the man who invented hankerchiefs, realized you could kill a thousand enemies with one blow?

I walking into a shop the other day. It said close the door behind you. I turned round and there wasn't one there

I was working as a sou chef in a fancy restaurant but I got sacked when they found out I wasn't an American Indian

When GW went to school his arithmetic skills were so poor, that they were considered weapons of Maths destruction

A gardener beat his wife into a brain dead pulp because he preferred vegetables to people

Ladies - eat, drink and be merry, for tomorrow you diet!

'Why are you shooting at my feet Marshall?'
'I like to see scum dancing'

STUPID JOKES FOR CLEVER PEOPLE
&
CLEVER JOKES FOR STUPID PEOPLE

I love Groundhog Day - I could watch it again and again, and again...

Life isn't what it used to be - it used to be treacle

Doctors diary entry for patient with penile dysfunction "Saw Willy - willy sore"

The Highlands of Scotland has its own version of 'Where's Wally' - it's called spot the dead sheep

'So Mr Michelin-man you're leaving after all this time? Well I hope you have a Goodyear when you re-tyre'

Message from the reindeers 'Don't feed the driver because Santa Claws'

Before enlightenment - wash dishes, sweep floor. After enlightenment, trick someone else into doing it.

Before enlightenment - chop water, wash in sticks. After enlightenment chop sticks, wash in water.

I had a fatwa put on me once. It weighed so much I wished it had been a thinwa instead.

Travel broadens the mind - sitting broadens the behind.

STUPID JOKES FOR CLEVER PEOPLE
&
CLEVER JOKES FOR STUPID PEOPLE

Police like jumpers - they're always pointing and shouting at drivers 'Pullover!'

Do hedgehogs suffer from prickly heat?

My son is a craven coward but I finally got him to make a stand. It's about this high and made out of wood

When a German shouts at me, I'm not sure if he's telling me off or asking me to ring the emergency services
'Nein, nein, nein!'

A man pushed his brother into a combine harvester. He was cut up about it afterwards but not as much as his brother.

The doctor told me that if I carried on with my present lifestyle I'd be dead in a week, so I stopped going out with his wife

I'll never work on a ship with a skeleton crew ever again! They're all a load of bone idle, spineless, numbskulls!

A bad doctors life is a series of missed-aches.

What was George Michael's defence, when he was caught in a public toilet? 'It won't happen again - it was just a flash in the pan'.

STUPID JOKES FOR CLEVER PEOPLE
&
CLEVER JOKES FOR STUPID PEOPLE

How can you spot a bitter Irishman? He's got a potato on his shoulder.

'I've got an Indian lawn'
'What do you mean?'
'It's patchy.'

Excerpt from West Side Story "I've just sat on a tin-tack and I can't help shouting - My rear! My rear!'

Slave market offer of the week - buy Wong get Juan free!

A bisexual murderer, who killed both his male and female lover, was found guilty and hanged - he swung both ways.

When it comes to alcohol consumption, Bud's weiser than either Becks or Miller

Since George Bush came to power is it true that the Americans swear at an oaf of allegiance?

A man was using a sledgehammer to smash a lump of concrete in his garden, when a friend turned up 'Come on, put your back into it! Give it some Bruce Forsyth and ignorance!'

'Hey Tom, it's raining - what should we do?'
'I don't know about you but I'm hopping into MacDonalds for a Mac, a Big Mac'

STUPID JOKES FOR CLEVER PEOPLE
&
CLEVER JOKES FOR STUPID PEOPLE

Notice over prophets door 'Staff wanted'

I entered a whipping competition the other day and was surprised to find a woman beat me

My husband is an animal! He drinks like a fish, eats like a horse and farts like an elephant!

I know a happy man who's just had a sex change operation. Up until that point he'd had a ball

I'm bipolar – I've visited both the Arctic and Antarctic

I was a vegetarian until I got fed up with trying to make ends meat

The navy has announced that it's had to make cuts on all equipment used in its undersea boats. From now on it will all be substandard

Superman has turned into a vampire – he's in the crypt tonight

'My wife got drunk in Ibiza. The following day we flew to Indonesia'
'Jakarta?'
'No, she was able to walk under her own steam'

Hi! I'm Ian Zane and this is my son. He's Ian Zane too!

STUPID JOKES FOR CLEVER PEOPLE
&
CLEVER JOKES FOR STUPID PEOPLE

I threw Keith Richard and Mick Jagger in the river. Then I threw Bryan Ferry in after them and he sank like a stone too

Great minds think alike – great bodies stink alike

I don't believe in domestic violence usually but since I got married, my wife is Beaton every day

Dr Jekyl woke up one morning with a turban on his head. He'd been up all night, playing Hyde and Sikh

As I said to my wife, if I'm so dumb why did you buy me a smart phone for Christmas?

I don't know if I'm the laziest man in the world or not because I couldn't be bothered to even enter that competition

I know a girl who's got athletes legs. One look at her and you want to run a mile

When in Rome, do as The Romans do. When in Glasgow do as you're bloody well told!

Did you hear about the woman who married a scruffy Arab because she liked shabby sheikh? According to Glasgow pickpockets, every McLeod has a silver lining

STUPID JOKES FOR CLEVER PEOPLE
&
CLEVER JOKES FOR STUPID PEOPLE

One thing a vampire should never say 'It's true, I'd stake my life on it!'

Is poorly made coffee grounds for divorce?

If someone from the town is called a townie, what do you call someone from the country?

Welsh drunks keep calm and carry Owen

In Essex all is lost – it's the blond leading the blond!

I can't stand Sacha Baron-Cohen, in fact I think I've got an 'Ali G' to him

My mother said I'd never fill my dad's boots, so I pulled down my trousers and proved her wrong

I've got a friend who's got bluetooth, one green and the rest are yellow

I've hit the bottle again, since reading about scrap metal merchants stealing train lines – it sent me right off the rails!

Leslie Neilsen is going to star in a Hollywood remake of The Full Monty. It's going to be called 'Naked Bum, Two and a Half'
'Oh look, there's a cow stuck in a snow drift!'
'Friesian?'
'It must be'

STUPID JOKES FOR CLEVER PEOPLE
&
CLEVER JOKES FOR STUPID PEOPLE

Jimmy Cagney found himself stuck on top of a fireman's ladder with nowhere else to go and a policeman below him
'Okay copper, if I'm going down, you're going down with me!'

'This bread and butter isn't working'
'Why do you think that is?'
"I don't know, maybe it's jammed'

I was going to go ice skating the other day but pulled out at the last minute – I got cold feet

When I was younger I used to eat bubble and squeak all day. Now I'm older, all I do is bubble and squeak all day

I called my son rubbish because I wanted him to be a household name when he grew up

If man was meant to fly, they wouldn't have invented airport taxes

I thought my sick pig was going to die and it did but then the butcher laid his hands on it, and it was cured

An owl's boyfriend was getting over familiar in a storm
'Knock it off – it's too wet to woo

STUPID JOKES FOR CLEVER PEOPLE
&
CLEVER JOKES FOR STUPID PEOPLE

Me and my next door neighbour get on like a house on fire. He burnt down mine, so I burnt down his!

If squirrels hoard things, are they nuts?

Do people who are as thick as two short planks, sleep like logs?

My wife bought me a book on Nihilism for Christmas
I said thanks for nothing

If an old man marries a child bride, he's called a cradle snatcher but does that make her a grave robber?

Robin Williams became a physicist and discovered the smallest thing in the universe – the nano-nano particle

A man visited his friend, a vet, who was dealing with a parasite infested dog.
'Hold on Dave, this shouldn't take long – in fact I'll be with you in two ticks

The thing to remember about constipation is that no matter how hard things seem at the time, they always work themselves out in the end

I saw Quasimodo the other day
'The bells, the bells – they make me deaf!'

STUPID JOKES FOR CLEVER PEOPLE
&
CLEVER JOKES FOR STUPID PEOPLE

'Try Smirnoff' I said

Sir Laurence Oliviers dog fell on hard times after it's master died 'Bonio, Bonio wherefort art thou Bonio?'

Did you hear about the religious nut who thought he was the object Jesus died on? Every time he ran across the road he shouted "Thank God I'm a-cross!"

What do burglars do in October, with some of the items they stole earlier in the year? They don't return the candle sticks but they always put the clocks back.

I was once treated for impotence but it didn't make a vas deferens.

I wanted to join a nudist colony but in the end I couldn't bare it

I thought I'd found Mr Right but I was Mrs Wrong!

Isn't it funny what they put in cigarettes nowadays? I was just thinking that the other day, when smoking one of my bedsits and hedges.

I made a sketch of Henry The Eighths favourite executioner – it was drawn, hung and quartered in

STUPID JOKES FOR CLEVER PEOPLE
&
CLEVER JOKES FOR STUPID PEOPLE

my local art gallery.

A father and son are arguing
'I fought two world wars for you, you ungrateful sod!'
'Yeh, and you lost them both'

Women have a soft spot for men - it's between their legs.
Men have a soft spot for women - it's between their ears.

Scottish murder website @GlasgowKnifemare /\- (That's forward slash, backward slash, sidewards slash)

'Hey Cilla, what did you think of our truck fest?'
'It was a lorra, lorra, lorries; Laurie'

I'm so confused by political correctness, that I can't tell Wright from Wong.

Glasses are a con trick that everyone can see through

Some people don't have the sense they were born with but collect it again on their way out

I thought that the Gaza Strip was what Wayne Rooney wore at football matches, until I tried Smirnoff

STUPID JOKES FOR CLEVER PEOPLE
&
CLEVER JOKES FOR STUPID PEOPLE

The trouble with wedding cake is that it always ends in tiers

Has a woman giving a Frenchman a blow job, got a frog in her throat?

Don't play cards with a pair of big cats - one will always be lion and the other's bound to be a cheetah

Joining The Common Market has left Britain on the road to Rouen

'I want you to send all these letters but hold back this one'
'But why?'
'Because I want them sent without McPhail'

In an Irish duel - will Patrick Kilmartin or Martin, Kilpatrick?

My old dogs an alcoholic - it whines all day and ails all night

I've got a sex mad car - it's always trying to mount the pavement

King Harold never had any use for archers, until a Norman bowman made him see his point

A tissue is to be sneezed at!

STUPID JOKES FOR CLEVER PEOPLE
&
CLEVER JOKES FOR STUPID PEOPLE

A friend of mine just got married. He met his wife while fishing on the canal – he caught her eye

It's the age of the train! The stone age

What do you say to someone outside a Star Wars convention, with gum in their mouth? 'Hiya Chewy!'

I've got a warped sense of humour. I stood too close to the fire when I was a child

I love karate black belts – that's the tenth Dan I've eaten today!

'Why are you walking funny?'
'Thongs aren't what they used to be'

I'd rather have my wife in the gym, than Jim in my wife

Did you hear about the woman who married a miser because she felt sorry for his money?

According to my mother I was never the same after the accident – I think she called it birth

'My cousin has a bad case of whicket keeper'
'Is it catching?'
'I believe so'

STUPID JOKES FOR CLEVER PEOPLE
&
CLEVER JOKES FOR STUPID PEOPLE

Life is like the Chinese water torture. It's just one drip after another, wearing your nerves down

I understand you can't talk about the casualty list for Afghanistan – is it because there's a Tally-ban?

I went to the doctor with severe stomach cramps. He insisted I had a cat scan. Pointless. I'd only eaten a hotdog

I wonder, do they call it plastic surgery because of how you pay or what you face looks like afterwards?

Dr Who's old dog attacked and savaged another dog, so he went to a scrapyard for a replacement. Luckily it was B9

'Why are you wearing a T-shirt with 81 on it?'
'I'm just showing my age'

I visited Ann Frank's house last year. I queued for 3 hours and she wasn't even in.

Scottish food has a high reputation, considering it's based on cereal - that's why it's called oat cuisine

Don't the Scots have funny names for places?
Kirkudbright is Kirkubree
Kirkaldy is Kirkuddy
and Glasgow is the pits

STUPID JOKES FOR CLEVER PEOPLE
&
CLEVER JOKES FOR STUPID PEOPLE

Practice safe sex – become a lesbian

My old car was like a washing machine – every time it hit ice, it went into a spin cycle

What are you likely to find, if you visit a retired shoe makers convention?
I don't know for sure but it sounds like a load of old cobblers

Why is it that when I'm joking, everybody takes me seriously – yet when I'm serious, everybody laughs at me?

I used to think depression ran in my family but now I realize that it slouches

I hate smoking – that's why I left the fire brigade

One man's meat is another man's poisson

Armadilloes may be dangerous but aardvarks never killed anyone

There has been a series of ladders stolen in the local area. Police have cautioned the public that if the trend continues, than steps will be taken

If you're searching for Superman in the streets of Metropolis, where are you most likely to find him?
Up Lois Lane

STUPID JOKES FOR CLEVER PEOPLE
&
CLEVER JOKES FOR STUPID PEOPLE

The trouble with being a genetically altered werewolf is that you're always running around in bear feet

People who engage in sexual intercourse, come to a sticky end

The reason GW's speechmaking has improved of late is that his dad sent him to Guantanamo Bay for electrocution lessons

If you're a turkey at Christmas, you're plucked!

I thought lapsang suchong was a small dog, until I tried Smirnoff

If you dance with Antonio Banderos, you know you've been Tangoed

Prostitutes believe that the customer should always come first

MI5 – all visitors must report to deception

Baker's keep calm and carry a scone

There are two reactions possible when something goes wrong
'I wonder why that happened?' and
'Work, damn you, work!'

Life is too short (by at least three inches)

STUPID JOKES FOR CLEVER PEOPLE
&
CLEVER JOKES FOR STUPID PEOPLE

I'm unpopular with girls (Billy no dates)

Handbag rage – Oh yeh, you and whose Armani?

Mercedes owners drive me round the Benz!

If Muslims pray to Mecca and it's in the wrong direction, is it a false salaam?

It doesn't mean you're crazy if you speak to yourself (but if you answer and don't realize who it is...)

I lost twenty pounds on the pickpocket diet!

Selfishness is a mine-field

I'm conventional – I'm the exception to the exception

I wonder if people in wheelchairs like getting pushed around by other people?

I'm paranoid. I don't have imaginary friends, I have imaginary enemies

Split personality? I thought everybody knew we had two I's?

Salad dressing? It's not rocket science!

STUPID JOKES FOR CLEVER PEOPLE
&
CLEVER JOKES FOR STUPID PEOPLE

A man finished his dinner, took off his shoe and threw it at the dog, who yelped in pain
'That really hit the spot!'

When I want to get into the loft, I stand on my step children

'Hi-ho silver and away!'
'Who was that masked man?'
'Don't you know? That was the loan arranger!'

What did the remote viewer say as he was leaving his friends house?
'Don't get up, I'll see myself out'

My wife's a magician. Every time I put money in front of her, it disappears!

Given the choice, I'd rather have a Happy Chris Moss, rather than a Sad Chris Moss!

'Is it snowing outside?'
'No mine Fuhrer - it's hail Hitler!"

STUPID JOKES FOR CLEVER PEOPLE
&
CLEVER JOKES FOR STUPID PEOPLE

FRANKENSTEIN JOKES

Frankenstein is a man after my own heart!

I'd give my right arm to work for Victor Frankenstein

Frankenstein has his fathers eyes

When Baron Frankenstein is working on a project, I like to give him a hand

Did you know that Baron Victor Frankenstein was the first person in the world to take body building seriously?

What did Baron Frankenstein do when someone caught him building a monster? He made a bolt for it!

Frankenstein liked laying his wife's head on his shoulders but the rest of her he just left in the fridge.

Frankensteins monster fell into a combine harvester. I really wanted to tell him I'd collected all the pieces but I just didn't have the heart

I like visiting Victor Frankenstein - he always keeps an eye out for me and is willing to give me a hand if I need it

STUPID JOKES FOR CLEVER PEOPLE
&
CLEVER JOKES FOR STUPID PEOPLE

Frankenstein doesn't know very much about female anatomy but he tries to keep a breast

I wouldn't say Frankensteins monster is stupid but it hasn't got the brains it was born with

Don't go to Victor Frankenstein for cosmetic surgery - he charges an arm and a leg

Igor, stop running your fingers through your hair! Put down that severed hand and use a comb like everyone else.

For some odd reason, the students of Heidelberg University live in fear, every time that Baron Frankenstein goes head-hunting.

What should you never say to Baron Frankenstein, if he jabs you in the kidneys?
'Hey cut that out!' because he will

Do you know why Baron Frankenstein chose the assistant he did?
Because he was always Igor to please.

Frankenstein's monster was shopping in the village. As he was about to leave the shop, the storekeeper shouted after him
'Hoy, you forgot your change!'
'Silly me, I'd forget my head if it wasn't screwed on!'

STUPID JOKES FOR CLEVER PEOPLE
&
CLEVER JOKES FOR STUPID PEOPLE

After arguing with his assistant about who should be used for what, Baron Frankenstein went back to his lab.
'Hey professor, whose body and whose brain you're going to use in your new experiment?'
'I'm sorry Igor but I've made my decision - the mind is Willis, even if the body is Meeks.'

'Is it true what they're saying about Baron Frankenstein , Tam?'
'Aye laddie! He's come all the way to Scotland to experiment on the clans. He started on the McPherson then he went onto the clan Macleod and he's now turned his attention on one final clan, too hideous to mention. In fact here comes the ugliest monster you'll ever see!'
'You don't mean-'
'Yes, The McBride of Frankenstein!'

Frankenstein's monster was involved in a serious road accident and lost its lower limbs. It was taken to court because of careless driving. Victor pleaded with the judge for a leaner sentence but he was adamant that the monster had to pay for his crime. 'Your arguments don't cut any ice here. In any case it doesn't have a leg to stand on'

Frankensteins monster is a great, big coward! In fact I've never seen such a gutless and spineless wonder.

Life is like Frankensteins Monster chasing the Wolfman - it's just one damned thing after another

The monster appeared on a talk show "Our next guest is Baron Frankensteins monster - let's give him a great big hand! Sorry, he's already got one!"

Frankensteins Favourite Songs:-
I can't get you out of my head
I left my heart in San Francisco
Wherever I lay my head, that's my home

VAMPIRE CONVERSATIONS

Things vampires would never say:-
'Oh look, there's Van Helsing - shall we say hello?'
'Fancy a steak?'
'More Garlic?'

What do vampires say when they meet?
'I haven't seen you in years - you haven't aged a bit!'
'Fancy stopping for a quick bite?'
'Nice tux!'

What do Count Dracula's victims say to him, when first introduced?
'I've been dying to meet you'

2 vampires were walking along the street . One asked the other how he was.
'Not too bad. Yourself?'
Oh, mustn't crumble'

CANNIBAL JOKES

What does a well off cannibal feed his dog? His pedigree chum.

What do cannibals call cars? Meals on wheels

Never ask a cannibal if he's on his last legs.

What do cannibals say to each other before starting a meal?
Bone appetite!

What do cannibals do when they can't eat someone just now? Freeze a jolly good fellow!

How do cannibals control amateur crime waves? By eating ham burglars

What did the lovesick cannibal cook sing to his complaining customers, when they said they were fed up with the same thing every day?
'I only have thighs for stew'

If you're in a cannibal restaurant and want to complain about your meal, who do you go to?
The head waiter of course!

What do cannibals like for their main meal of the day?
Kate and Sidney pie

Cannibal - I've had my five a day

ZOMBIE JOKES

'I saw you throw salt on that zombie, to make him return to the grave - what did you put on him to make him get up in the first place?'
'Self-raising flour'

What do zombies eat for a treat?
Rowntrees Fruit Pustules

What do you say to a hungry zombie on a diet?
Eat your heart out!

RIDDLES

Why is Germany like a dog blanket?
Because it is unnaturally full of hairs!

STUPID JOKES FOR CLEVER PEOPLE
&
CLEVER JOKES FOR STUPID PEOPLE

A Klu Klux Klan member was asked where he stood on black people?
"The testicles usually"

Why should you never give new things to the Welsh?
Because they Wrexham!

What was on Aran before Goat Fell? Goat standing up.

Why can't Sir Ranulph Fiennes drink milk?
Because he's lack-toes intolerant

What do you get if you cross cattle with spaniels?
Nothing – it was a cocker-bull story

What's the difference between a man who runs a chocolate factory and a man with a bent penis?
One's Willy Wonka and the other's got a wonky willy

What do you get if you cross a religious group that plays musical instruments with one that is 200 years out of date?
The Salvation Amish

Which Irishman is always drunk?
Luke O'Zade

Did you hear about the cannibal's wife?
Henrietta!

STUPID JOKES FOR CLEVER PEOPLE
&
CLEVER JOKES FOR STUPID PEOPLE

What do you get if you swop the first letters of a famous Welsh singer's name?
Dame Burly Chassis

Why do dogs have runny noses?
Because they cannot keep up with them if they walk

Where does an Irish rocket science live?
In County Down of course!

What happens when you throw a Scotsman on a fire?
I don't know for sure but I think Robbie Burns

Why should people who steal cattle, not wear paper trousers?
Because it is easy to catch them rustling

Which strange shaped cowboy fell off his horse?
Oblong Cassidy

What did the man hiding in the trenches, say to the sniper?
'We haven't seen each other for a while – did you miss me?'

What do you get if you cross a Russian woman with a means of transport?
Anya bike!

STUPID JOKES FOR CLEVER PEOPLE
&
CLEVER JOKES FOR STUPID PEOPLE

What do you call a German who sits on your head?
Helmut

Why is an electrical engineer like Professor Moriarty?
They're both desperate to get ohms

What do you call a Russian, who can't control his enthusiasm?
A Serge of optimisim

What did Wagner shout, when he hit his thumb with a hammer?
'Gotterdammerung!'

What do you get if you cross a muck spreader with George Elliot?
Silage Marner

What's the similarity between a Native American tribe and a Chinaman, singing in the style of a blackman?
One is Rapper Ho and the other's Arapaho too

Why did the fat woman throw Keith Richard out the window?
Because she wanted to lose a stone

What does a posh woman say, when she tickles her baby under the chin?
'Gucci, Gucci, Goo!'

STUPID JOKES FOR CLEVER PEOPLE
&
CLEVER JOKES FOR STUPID PEOPLE

What's the difference between a famous children's writer and a flattened breakfast cereal?
One is Roald Dahl and the other is rolled oats

Why was Hitler no good at golf?
Because he was always stuck in the bunker at the end of his game

Why was the spirit that possessed a body, confident of winning its court case?
Because it knew possession was nine tenth's of the law

Which film star turned a funny colour when they died?
Mickey Marooney

If you run out of nan bread, what can you use as a substitute?
Grandad bread of course!

Why is Darth Vader so angry?
Because he's got 'only one Kenobi'

What do policemen say to Collared Doves?
'You're nicked!"

How can you tell a Tibetan Cockerel that's a cross-dresser?
Because him-a-laya

STUPID JOKES FOR CLEVER PEOPLE
&
CLEVER JOKES FOR STUPID PEOPLE

What pop group made a stand against racism?
The White Cliffs of Dover.

What do you get if you cross Taggart with The Lord of the Rings?
There's been a murder in Mordor

What do you get if you cross a gangster with counterfeit money?
Hit on the head and dumped in the river

What do you get if you cross Naomi Campbell with a dinosaur?
Model behaviour

In what way did Robert Newton, the actor, show his relationship to the physicist of the same name?
After drinking all night, he demonstrated the effects of gravity.

Who was sacked from children's TV because of his drinking?
Thomas the tanked-up engine

What's the difference between a thorn in Henry the second's side and a pale imitation?
One's Thomas-a-Becket and the other's Thomas a bucket

Why did the happy man rob a bank? Because he felt like a million dollars!

STUPID JOKES FOR CLEVER PEOPLE
&
CLEVER JOKES FOR STUPID PEOPLE

Why do investment bankers like miniature kitchen tools?
Because they don't like big whisks

Why is a proctologist like an astronomer?
Because he's only interested in Uranus

Which French philosopher throws terror into everyone's hearts, when he enters the room?
Jean Paul Fartre - he's known for kicking up a stink wherever he goes!

What did the leader of an expedition, carrying out an experiment on hibernation, say at the start of it?
'Okay people. let's get this snow on the toad!'

What did King Canute say to his adoring people, when he was trying to prove that he was as vulnerable as they were to life's disasters?
'See how my tea has fallen?'

What did Ranulph Fiennes sing to himself as he dragged his sleigh through the icy wastes? 'To - To - Tootsies, goodbye!'

Why don't people with Thalidomide use handguns? Because they have trouble with small arms

What did the werewolf bride say to her husband on their wedding night? Just a second honey - I'm changing!

STUPID JOKES FOR CLEVER PEOPLE
&
CLEVER JOKES FOR STUPID PEOPLE

What did Elvis say when he realized he'd been reincarnated as a Bottle of Coke?
"Aha, wow yeh - I'm all shook up!"

Why did the tenpin not like living in an arab country?
Because he was always being stood up on dates for a laugh

What did the Bible-thumping sports master always carry with him?
Cane and a ball

Why did everybody in the directors box of the best football club in the Scottish Highlands collapse, when the sickly astrologer brought in a friend?
Because of Super Caley's, fragile mystic's, ex-pals halitosis

What do you say if a gunman bursts into your house - shoots your mother, shoots your father and then shoots you?
'Ma! Pa! Ouch!'

What do you say if a gunman bursts into your house and shoots your mother, your father then ET?
'Ma! Pa! Ouch!

What do you get if you cross a black actress with the Lockerbie bomber?
Angela Bassett Megrahi

STUPID JOKES FOR CLEVER PEOPLE
&
CLEVER JOKES FOR STUPID PEOPLE

What do you get if you further cross the result?
Angela Bassett-Hound Megrahi

What do most people not like seeing on their toast?
Middle age spread

Why did the chicken cross the road?
'Coz the coward didn't have the guts to walk passed me!

What do you get if you cross a railway line with a tortoise?
Hit by a train

Why do men treat women as objects? Because their objective is objectionable!

Why do some people like saying hello?
It's just part of their 'Hiya!' nature

What's the definition of weightlifting?
A fat man getting out of bed

How do you know if the person at the other end of the bar, drinking beer is a scientist or not?
They'll only be interested in Coors and effect.

How do you know if the guy behind you on the highway is a grammarian?
He'll only be interested in parsing.

STUPID JOKES FOR CLEVER PEOPLE
&
CLEVER JOKES FOR STUPID PEOPLE

How can you be sure an ophthalmologist is going to see you arriving at his house?
Because he'll keep an eye out for you.

What is a pirate's favourite computer?
an I-Patch

How can you tell if a schizophrenic is in a bad mood?
He won't even speak to himself.

What do composers carry with them to the supermarket ?
Their Chopin Lizsts

How do you kill a Mexican?
Through Manuel strangulation

What do you call old golfers?
Tee Wrecks

What do you get if you cross an Australian marsupial with a tragic Greek king?
Platypus Rex.

Why did the policeman with the bad heart fail to leave the hospital?
Because he arrested on the way out.

Why are anteaters very healthy?
Because they only eat the freshest new-tree ants.

STUPID JOKES FOR CLEVER PEOPLE
&
CLEVER JOKES FOR STUPID PEOPLE

Why did the locals desert the pub in droves, when the pig farmers came into town?
Because nobody likes Ham Chewers night.

What should you never say to an angler at a VD clinic?
Caught anything lately?

What drink does King John detest since signing The Magna Carte?
Runny Mead

I know an art dealer who thought Picasso's work was utter rubbish and wouldn't stock it in his gallery. He's laughing on the other side of his face now!

I bought a memory foam mattress topper but can't remember if I put it on the bed or not?

FILMS THAT NEVER GOT MADE

'I Spit on your Gravy!' - A sordid tale of a chefs revenge

'Dead on a Rival' - Husband having heart attack when he catches his wife with her lover

'Dracula, prints of Darkness' - More holiday snaps ruined by incompetent developers

STUPID JOKES FOR CLEVER PEOPLE
&
CLEVER JOKES FOR STUPID PEOPLE

'A Womb with a View' - A Gynaecologist on a bus man's holiday

'Buckfast at Tiffany's' - Cheap British remake of Audrey Hepburn classic

'A Fistful of Donuts' and 'For a Few Donuts More' - The life of a fast food junkie

'Whoops Apocalypso!'/'Apocalypso now' - Jamaican remakes of more famous titles

'What's Doug got to do with it?' - The argumentative lives of Ike and Tina Turner

'Planet of the Grapes' - Follow up to 'Attack of the Tomato Men'

'Retch for the Sky' – A pilot not quite made of the right stuff

'And then there were some' - The cowardly remake of an Agatha Christie film

'The Ego has Landed' – Donald Trump's attempt to build a golf course in Scotland

STUPID JOKES FOR CLEVER PEOPLE
&
CLEVER JOKES FOR STUPID PEOPLE

BOOK TITLES

'Open a Box of Scorpions' by Celia Fate

'What's the Answer?' by Ida No

'Keeping your grass short' by Lorna Mower

'How to murder your husband' by Evelyn Tent

'You just can't win' by Noah Vale

'Caught short' by Bob's Down and DeWitt

'Get your clothes on, you're nicked!' by Yvonne Jeans

'Lost on the Continent' by Frances Diswaye

'What a bunch of Losers!' by Hugh and Millie Asian

'Is it Bad News? by Terry Bull

'Sexual Organs' by Jenny Taylor

'The Lazy man's guide to life' by Bo Nidel

'American TV Crime Shows' by Ellie Law

'Compulsive Gaming' by Mustafa Go

STUPID JOKES FOR CLEVER PEOPLE
&
CLEVER JOKES FOR STUPID PEOPLE

'American Indian weapons of mass destruction' by Tommy Hawk and A. Spear

'How to start an argument' by I.M. Wright & U.R. Wong.

'Juan in a Million' - Mexican version of 'Where's Wally?'

'Another Name for Sex' by Willy Duncan

NAMES SERIES

Just because my name is Matt, doesn't mean you can walk all over me

Just because my name is Stew, doesn't mean I'm going to let you bite my dumplings

Just because my name's Eve, doesn't mean I was born yesterday

Just because my name's David, doesn't mean I've got Goliath in my trousers

Just because my name is Moses, don't think I'll take you to the promised land

Just because my name is Rob, doesn't mean I'm going to take you for every penny you own

STUPID JOKES FOR CLEVER PEOPLE & CLEVER JOKES FOR STUPID PEOPLE

Just because my name is Rich, doesn't mean I am

Just because my name is Dick, doesn't mean my surname is Head

Just because my name is Owen, doesn't mean I feel indebted to you

Just because my name is Frank, doesn't mean I don't tell porkies

Just because my name is Diane, doesn't mean I'm dying to meet you

Just because my name is Helen, doesn't mean my surname is Earth

Just because my name is Barbara, doesn't mean I come from Seville

Just because my name is Doug, doesn't mean I dig you

T-SHIRT DESIGNS

Official translator – I speak Glaswegian

I'm Immortal! (up till now)

STUPID JOKES FOR CLEVER PEOPLE
&
CLEVER JOKES FOR STUPID PEOPLE

I went to Africa and all I've got to show for it is a dose of malaria

Are you deaf? I don't need a hearing aid!

I'm happy - Mahmood is good!

I hate work! (It gets in the way of my social life)

Prejudice is a fashion statement

Reality doesn't take prisoners

How did you know I was Australian? (Written upside-down)

There's nothing like death for sobering you up

Where would I be without me?

One man's meet is another man's bugger off!

Aged to prefection (but just turning rancid)

Mad scientist (leave me a clone!)

I'm the only grey in the village

There's no excuse for real life

I'm keeping up a brave front, considering what's going on behind my back!

Only a fool who's fooling himself, can fool another fool!

Give me Liberty's or give me De'Ath's!

I have nothing to say but that I have nothing to say (and I can see no point in telling you that there is no point in telling you this)

DEVIL'S DICTIONARY

Government - agency that comes to power, claiming to solve all of society's ills, then refuses to on the grounds it will put it out of a job (any similar agency working this way e.g's educational establishments that promote ignorance/ hospitals that make you sicker than when you went in)

Cellfie – camera phone dedicated to taking photos of yourself in exotic locations, while obscuring more interesting subjects behind you, hidden by your fat head.

Arrogance - stupidity disguised as insanity

Conservative - labour saving device

Weightlifting - fat man getting out of bed

Soul mate - person you want to spend the rest of

your life with
Sole mate - person you are forced to put up with because nobody else wants you

Odd - creator of a new fashion
Normal - follower of fashion

Defiant - wants what they want - not what I want to give them

Zombie – creature smelling of rotting flesh, that stumbles around, staring into space and lusting after young bodies aka a dirty old man

Family Friendly – B&B packed full of screaming kids

DAFT DEFINITIONS

Mammygram - x-ray to see if you're turning into Al Jolson

Burglar Alarm - clock set to wake tired burglars on night shift, by kind residents who want them to break into their homes on time ('Where is that burglar? I'm going to be late for the concert again!')

Ashburgers Syndrome - idiot who should never be left alone with a barbie

STUPID JOKES FOR CLEVER PEOPLE
&
CLEVER JOKES FOR STUPID PEOPLE

Wet – Prince Philip's reply to a question he didn't quite understand

Hand made - artificially inseminated.

Self-made man (see above)

Copracide - fan who died when shit hit him

Matricide - person suffocated to death by a bed

PLACE NAMES

Doomray - power station near John O'Groats in Scotland

'What do you think of the wind in the Western Isles Angus?'
'You get Uist to it'

You have to keep your head down in Scotland's biggest city bars - Glass come, glass go

QUOTES

'As the Shellfish find - Conches makes Cowries of us All' (William Shakeshell)

As an old fossil will tell you, there's no fuel like an old fuel

Ego only knows one note - Me, me, me, me!

Life is like sex - full of ups and downs, ins and outs and side to sides

Do vampire policeman like to go on stake-outs?

OBITUARIES

Deforest Kelly deforested (Bones is now, well bones)

Death of The Fiddler on the Roof star, after long illness - Topol, over

Actor from The Lord of the Rings Trilogy dies - Andy says goodbye to the Serkis
(Gollum but not forgotten)

Last of the Summer Wine star, Bill Owen, kicks the bucket - Compo's in the compost

STUPID JOKES FOR CLEVER PEOPLE
&
CLEVER JOKES FOR STUPID PEOPLE

INDEX

If I couldn't be bothered to write an introduction, what makes you think I'd bother with an index for a joke book of all things?

STUPID JOKES FOR CLEVER PEOPLE
&
CLEVER JOKES FOR STUPID PEOPLE

NOTE

If you simply hated this book, you won't want to know about my Pinterest board below either but being a sadist, I thought I'd drop a link anyway

www.pinterest.com/paigetheoracle/shallow-humour

That's '*oracle,*' not '*coracle*' as I don't believe in boats for women

STUPID JOKES FOR CLEVER PEOPLE
&
CLEVER JOKES FOR STUPID PEOPLE

www.ingramcontent.com/pod-product-compliance
Lightning Source LLC
Chambersburg PA
CBHW050040080526
44586CB00014B/1394